What's Awake?

Bats

Patricia Whitehouse

www.raintreepublishers.co.uk

Visit our website to find out more information about Raintree books.

To order:

☎ Phone +44 (0) 1865 888066

▤ Fax +44 (0) 1865 314091

▣ Visit www.raintreepublishers.co.uk

Raintree is an imprint of Capstone Global Library Limited, a company incorporated in England and Wales having its registered office at 7 Pilgrim Street, London, EC4V 6LB - Registered company number: 6695582

Edited by Adrian Vigliano and Diyan Leake
Designed by Joanna Hinton-Malivoire
Picture research by Tracy Cummins
Originated by Chroma Graphics (Overseas) Pte Ltd
Printed in China by South China Printing Company Ltd

ISBN 978 1 4062 1237 2 (hardback)
14 13 12 11 10
10 9 8 7 6 5 4 3 2 1

ISBN 978 1 4062 1242 6 (paperback)
14 13 12 11 10
10 9 8 7 6 5 4 3 2 1

British Library Cataloguing in Publication Data

Whitehouse, Patricia, 1958-
  Bats. - 2nd ed. - (What's awake?)
  1. Bats - Juvenile literature 2. Nocturnal animals - Juvenile literature
  I. Title
  599.4

Acknowledgements

We would like to thank the following for permission to reproduce photographs: AP Photo p. **9** (© Jun Dumaguing); Getty Images pp. **5** (© Regis Martin), **8** (© Bob Elsdale), **10** (© John Downer), **11** (© Theo Allofs), **13** (© Tim Laman), **15** (© Tim Laman); Jupiter Images p. **22** (© Bernhard Volmer); Minden Pictures p. **14** (© Michael Durham); National Geographic Stock p. **6** (Minden Pictures/© Michael Durham); Photo Researchers Inc. pp. **7** (© Bat Conservation International/Dr. Merlin D. Tuttle), **17** (© Merlin D. Tuttle, Bat Conservation International), **20** (© Stephen J. Krasemann); Photolibrary p. **21** (© Densey Clyne); Shutterstock pp. **4** (© photobank), **16** (© Eduard Kyslynskyy), **19** (© Alin Andrei), **23a** (© George Burba), **23b** (© Ra'id Khalil), **23c** (© Martin Wall), **23d** (© TheSupe87), **23e** (© Laurence Gough); Visuals Unlimited p. **18** (© Jack Milchanowski).

Cover photograph reproduced with permission of Minden Pictures (© Richard Du Toit). Back cover photograph of a bat colony reproduced with permission of Photolibrary (© George Burba) and of fur reproduced with permission of Photolibrary (© Eduard Kyslynskyy).

Every effort has been made to contact copyright holders of material reproduced in this book. Any omissions will be rectified in subsequent printings if notice is given to the publisher.

 CAUTION: Remind children that it is not a good idea to handle wild animals. Children should wash their hands with soap and water after they touch any animal.

Contents

Some words are shown in bold, **like this**. You can find them in the picture glossary on page 23.

What's awake?

Some animals are awake when you go to sleep.

Animals that stay awake at night are **nocturnal**.

Bats are awake at night.

What are bats?

Bats can fly, but they are not birds.

Bats are mammals.

baby bat

Mammals have **fur** on their bodies.

Mammals make milk for their babies.

What do bats look like?

wing

Bats have **fur** on their bodies.

They have two wings covered with skin.

Some bats are as small as a thumb.

Other bats have wings as wide as a person's arms.

Where do bats live?

Bats' homes are called **roosts**.

They live in groups called **colonies**.

In the wild, bats live in caves or trees.

In cities, bats live under roofs
or bridges.

What do bats do at night?

Bats wake up just before dark.

They start to move around and fly.

They fly away to look for food.

Bats can eat all night.

What do bats eat?

Most bats eat moths.

They eat other insects, too.

Many bats eat fruit.

This bat is eating a fruit called a fig.

What do bats sound like?

Bats make two kinds of sounds.

One is a squeaking sound.

The other sound helps bats to find food.

Scientists need to use machines to hear this sound.

How are bats special?

Bats use a special sound to help them find insects.

The sound bounces off the insects, so the bat can tell where they are.

Bats hang upside down to sleep.

Where do bats go during the day?

In the morning, bats fly back to their **roosts**.

baby bats

Bats look after their babies.

Then, they go to sleep.

Bat map

wings

fur

Picture glossary

 **colony** group of bats

 **fur** soft hair that some animals have on their bodies

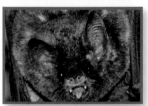 **nocturnal** awake at night

 **roost** place where bats rest and have their families

 **scientist** person who learns about animals and other things in nature

Index

Note to parents and teachers

Reading for information is an important part of a child's literacy development. Learning begins with a question about something. Help the children think of themselves as investigators and researchers by encouraging their questions about the world around them. In this book, the animal is identified as a mammal. A mammal by definition is one that is covered with hair or fur, and feeds its young with milk from its body. Point out the fact that, although the animal in this book is a mammal, many other animals are mammals – including humans.